The Lord is my Shepherd, but...

The Lord is my Shepherd, but...

Confessions of the Natural Man

by **BARBARA JURGENSEN**

Illustrations by Robin Jensen

ZONDERVAN PUBLISHING HOUSE
Grand Rapids, Michigan

THE LORD IS MY SHEPHERD, BUT . . .
Copyright © 1969 by Zondervan Publishing House
Grand Rapids, Michigan
Library of Congress Catalog Card Number 69-11656

Second printing January 1970
Third printing September 1970
Fourth printing January 1971
Fifth printing   August 1971

Printed in the United States of America

There may be a little of the natural man
in some of us.

ACKNOWLEDGMENTS

A thank you is hereby given to the following magazines in which the articles included here have appeared:

Christian Century

Christian Living

Churchmen

Conquest

Contact

Frontiers

Greater Works

High

Light and Life Evangel

Lutheran Herald

Lutheran Standard

Lutheran Women

The Mennonite

One

Teen Time

War/Peace Report

Youth's Christian Companion

CONTENTS

The Natural Man Misses the Whole Idea
THE LORD IS MY SHEPHERD, BUT 11

The Natural Man Sends His Regrets
I'M SORRY WE'VE OUTGROWN YOU, GOD 14

The Natural Man Wrings His Hands
I'M READY TO PUSH THE PANIC BUTTON 17

The Natural Man Gives Up
I CAN'T FIND GOD 20

Natural Men Lament Their Situation Down
Through the Ages
IT'S TOO HARD TO BE A CHRISTIAN! 22

The Natural Man Makes a Discovery
CHRISTIANITY DOESN'T WORK 25

The Natural Man Protests
YOU DIDN'T HAVE TO MAKE LIFE SO HARD, GOD 29

The Natural Man Speaks His Mind
I DON'T LIKE THE CROSS 32

The Natural Man Through the Week
I DON'T HAVE TIME TO READ THE BIBLE 34

The Natural Man Asks
WHY SHOULD I PRAISE GOD? 36

The Natural Man Puffs Up With Pride
IF ONLY EVERYONE WERE LIKE ME 38

The Natural Man Examines His Status
I DESERVE ALL I HAVE 40

The Natural Man Gives Himself a Pat on the Back
IN PRAISE OF NORTHERN VIRTUE 43

The Natural Man Points a Finger
THOSE MONKS! 44

The Natural Man Speaks Out
THE NATURAL MAN TAKES UP HIS CROSS . . . SORT OF . .46

A Perspective on Race
    THE NATURAL MAN SOLVES THE RACE PROBLEM 48

The Natural Man's Mind Wanders
    I SAY THE APOSTLES' CREED IN CHURCH 50

The Natural Man Gets One-Upped
    THE SPECTER AND I 52

The Natural Man Admits a Few Things
    JESUS' LIFE MIGHT HAVE GONE SOMETHING LIKE
    THIS IF HE HAD BEEN MORE LIKE ME 55

The Natural Man's Prayers Clog the Computers
    THE INTERNATIONAL GEOPRAYERICAL YEAR 56

The Natural Woman Saves Wear and Tear on Her Bible
    THE DAY MRS. SHRDLU FUMBLED HER
    FEATHERDUSTER 60

The Natural Man Makes Another Discovery
    WHEN THE WHAT IS CALLED UP YONDER 63

The Natural Man Gets His Come-Uppance
    THE EMPTY CHAIR AFFAIR 67

*The Natural Man Begins to Appreciate the
Privilege of Praying*
    I HAD A LITTLE TROUBLE PRAYING 72

The Natural Man Shudders at Man's Inhumanity
    NUCLEAR THOUGHT 76

The Natural Man Makes Another Discovery
    HIGH NOON IN HEAVEN 78

The Natural Man Puts His Feet in Someone Else's Shoes
    BLACK THOUGHT 82

*The Natural Man Remembers the Russian Astronaut's
Report That He Did Not Find God in Outer Space*
    OUR FATHER WHO ART 84

The Natural Man Realizes His Imperfections
    EIGHT YEARS AS A THIRD CORNET 86

The Natural Man Discovers God
    THE INCIDENT AT ST. DUTY'S 90

The Lord
is my
Shepherd,
but...

The natural man
misses the whole idea

THE LORD IS MY SHEPHERD, BUT . . .

The Lord is my shepherd
But Lord, You know I don't have time today for You to lead me. Perhaps tomorrow. Or the next day.

I shall not want
I know that I don't actually want for the necessities of life, Lord, but there are so many things I could use — my own TV, for instance, and an outboard motor, and a bigger bank account. Come to think of it, there are a lot of things I want!

He maketh me to lie down in green pastures
In green pastures! I certainly don't have the time to go out and lie down in some grassy meadow.

He leadeth me beside the still waters
A pleasant enough phrase. I hope that some day in heaven I'll take just such a walk with You, Lord. But You know how it is here — a million things to do all the time . . .

He restoreth my soul
He what? Oh, restoreth — like when you take an old chest

11

DON'T BOTHER ME GOD I'M BUSY!

of drawers and refinish it so you can use it some more. That's a lot of work, isn't it? Well, if You want to, go ahead, Lord. But I can just as well keep on using my soul the way it is.

He leadeth me in the paths of righteousness for his name's sake

I'm all for righteousness, Lord, but I have so many other things to do. Could we postpone this little jaunt for a while?

Yea though I walk through the valley of the shadow of death, I will fear no evil: for thou art with me

You will be with me, won't You, Lord? I can't go through that all by myself!

Thy rod and thy staff they comfort me

How about a little more staff and a little less rod? What are You trying to make me into — a saint?

Thou preparest a table before me in the presence of my enemies

So far it's been me watching my enemies feasting and making merry. Let's show them!

Thou anointest my head with oil

What for?

My cup runneth over

Actually, there are a few more things I would like that I forgot to mention — my own car, a lot more clothes, a trip to Hawaii . . .

Surely goodness and mercy shall follow me all the days of my life: and I will dwell in the house of the Lord forever.

I'm kind of busy right now, Lord — but You will save room for me, won't you?

The natural man
sends his regrets

I'm Sorry We've Outgrown You, God

You see, it's been a long time since You created the world, God, and in that time man has really advanced scientifically. We've discovered the 103 elements . . .

> VOICE: *The 103 elements . . . I made a few more than that. Keep looking.*

And we've split the atom, unlocking the greatest power in the universe . . .

> *Unlocking the greatest power in the universe! You've only just begun to turn the key! And the greatest power in the universe may be something else again: you've barely begun to release the power of My Spirit and My love into the world.*

And just look at how we're conquering space!

> *Conquering space? Some day, when you build a telescope about a dozen times as powerful as the largest one you now have, take it out on your fastest space ships to the farthest planet you can reach, and have a look at what's beyond.*

And think of how we're defeating the major diseases! Every year we find new cures!

And Who do you think it is that heals your diseases?

And consider what we've done in the field of human relations! Think of how barbaric man used to be, and of how civilized he is now. We don't need the Ten Commandments any more; man has grown up and can take care of himself.

From My vantage point I can see everything that's going on at this present moment in the world. Would you like to come up and observe what civilized man is doing?

And we have psychiatrists now who are able to help us deal with our problems. So I think you can see, God, why it would be foolish and out of date for us to pay much attention to You any more. I'm sorry that it has to be this way, but that's progress.

The natural man
wrings his hands

I'm Ready to Push the Panic Button

There are so many things to cause anxiety today that I can hardly go on living! Like the bomb . . . the bomb could fall any minute!

    VOICE: *Mankind has always lived under the threat of destruction, whether from prehistoric clubs or medieval crossbows or modern nuclear pyrotechnics. But . . .*

And the Communists could take us over any day!

    Man has always had to live with the possibility that another tribe might overcome his. But I . . .

And automation could suddenly wipe out whatever job I train for!

    This business of earning a living has always been a precarious thing at best. But I am . . .

And think of the horrible crimes being committed lately! None of us is safe!

    Has man ever been safe? But I am with . . .

And of the terrible diseases!

WHY CAN'T THE WORLD BE SAFE FOR ME, GOD ?

Sickness we have always had with us. But I am with you . . .

And of all the racial troubles! How do we know that one of these days the oppressed races won't rise up and overthrow us?

You don't know. It would be terrifying if they started doing to you what you've been doing to them. But I am with you always.

And this interplanetary business — what if we should be invaded by another planet?

Well, your country's planning to drop in on them as soon as you can. Should they be worrying about that? But remember, I am with you always . . .

Well, it's all too much for me. If it weren't for tranquilizers and TV, I would have pushed the panic button long ago.

I am with you always, even until the end of the world.

The natural man
gives up

I Can't Find God

The natural man in Abraham's time: How does a person find God? I hear He spoke to Abraham the other day, promising him that the Messiah will come. But just hearing God *speak* wouldn't be enough for me. I'd have to *see* Him. If I could live long enough to *see* the Messiah, then I could believe.

The natural man in Jesus' time: They say this is the Messiah, but how do I know He really is? Just *seeing* Him doesn't help me know. Why doesn't God *speak* and *tell* me that this is His Son? Then I could believe.

The natural man today: If I could have lived back in the time of Abraham and could have *heard* God speaking directly to me, then I'm sure I could believe. Or if I could have lived in the time of Jesus and could have *seen* Him. But how can I believe today when I can't *see* Him or *hear* Him?

IT SURE IS TOUGH TO BELIEVE IN GOD !

*Natural men
lament their situation
down through the ages*

It's Too Hard to Be a Christian!

64 A.D. *Nero persecutes the Christians in Rome:*
How can I be a Christian with such persecution going on?

302 A.D. *Diocletian throws Christians to the lions:*
I can't possibly follow Christ in these terrible days!

546 A.D. *The Goths invade Italy:*
The heathen have overrun us! Christianity can never survive. I can't be a Christian in a situation like this!

711 A.D. *The Moors conquer Spain:*
Mohammedanism will annihilate Christianity! We can't possibly hold out against these fanatical followers of Mohammed. It's too hard to live a Christian life in these times!

1074 A.D. *The Turks seize and sack Jerusalem:*
The very center of Christianity has been captured and destroyed! I see no future now but the gradual decline

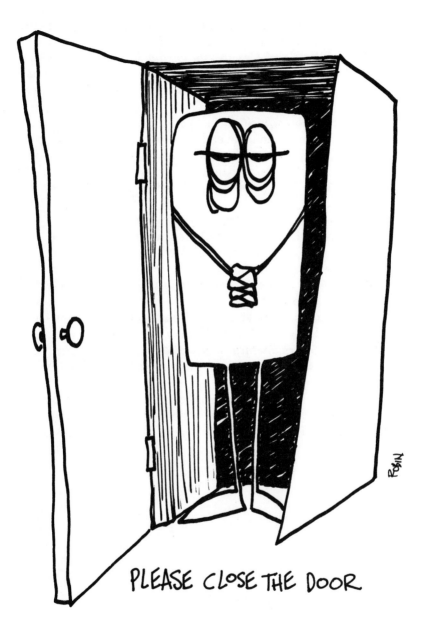

PLEASE CLOSE THE DOOR

and the eventual extinction of Christianity. I can't even hope to be a Christian any more.

1346 A.D. *Battle of Crecy; gunpowder first used in Europe:*
How can mankind and Christianity continue in the face of so devastating a weapon? It's impossible to keep on being a Christian.

1483 A.D. *The Inquisition in Spain:*
The Church can never bear up under such a flagrant misuse of the teachings of Christ — seeking out and killing unbelievers and heretics. It will falter and fall. I don't see how I can live a Christian life in these horrible days.

1665 A.D. *The Great Plague of London:*
Thousands are dying! There's never been a more difficult time in which to live! How can anyone expect me to be a Christian now?

1861 A.D. *Six states secede from the Union, the Confederacy is formed:*
In a nation wracked by strife and civil war, how can I possibly live a Christian life?

1970 A.D. *Interplanetary exploration, automation, interracial strife, the world divided into two camps, the threat of nuclear war:*
Has there ever been a more difficult time in which to be a Christian? It's impossible to be a Christian at a time like this!

The natural man
makes a discovery

CHRISTIANITY DOESN'T WORK

You can say what you want about Christianity, but I've tried it, and it doesn't work.

VOICE: *Tell me about it.*

Well, take for instance this matter of turning the other cheek when somebody does you wrong. I tried that the other day. This fellow and I collided going into the bank. I picked up his hat and handed it to him and apologized for bumping into him.

What did he do? He grabbed his hat out of my hand and snarled, "Idiot!"

Then when we were both at the desk in the center of the lobby making out deposit slips, his fountain pen wasn't working right. So where did he shake it? Toward me. Ink all over my coat sleeve.

I was pretty mad, but then I decided now would be the time to practice turning the other cheek. So I said nothing about the ink all over my sleeve. Instead I offered him the

I'M GLAD I ONLY HAVE TWO CHEEKS!

use of my pen. Furious, he wadded up his deposit slip and threw it into my face? My cheek smarted for a while.

Wait — I never said that if you turned the other cheek, other people would treat you well in return.

Or take this business about going the second mile. I decided to try that too. The other day as I was driving along a country road, I came to a fellow standing beside his car.

"I'm out of gas. Can you give me a lift to the gas station half a mile down the road?" he asked.

"Sure," I said. "Hop in."

So he got the gas and I drove him back to his car. Then he remembered that his spare was flat and asked if I would take it back to the station and get it fixed while he put the gas into his tank. I decided that this was a real chance for me to go the second mile, so I said "Sure" and drove off to the station.

When I came back with the repaired tire (which I had paid to have fixed), he threw it into his trunk, yelled "Thanks, sucker," and roared off.

I never implied that if you went the second mile, you would be rewarded — or even treated fairly — by the person you helped.

Or take the matter of if anyone would take your coat, let him have your cloak as well. A week or two ago I was at a convention. After dinner when I went out to the hall to get my top coat, there was this other fellow putting it on. So I said, "Hey, that's *my* coat!"

He said, "No, it's mine."

Well, I knew I had put it at the end of that particular rack and that mine had a rip in the shoulder seam right where this one did. Then I remembered that I'd left my black gloves in the right hand pocket.

"All right then," I said to him, "without looking, what's in the right pocket?"

He looked indignant for a moment, then reached in and

pulled out the gloves. "My gloves," he replied, holding them up.

I thought again. *What was in the left hand pocket?* Then I remembered. A road map of the province of Manitoba.

"All right now," I said, "without reaching in, what's in the left pocket?"

"Look!" he said, nearing the boiling point, "I don't have time for games!"

"Well," I said, "if there's a map of Manitoba in there, that's my coat!" I reached into the pocket and pulled out the map.

"All right," I said. "Give me my coat."

"It's mine," he insisted and walked off.

Now *I* was near the boiling point. But then the thought struck me: now that he had taken my coat, as a Christian I should offer him my cloak.

Having no cloak to offer, but wanting to fulfill at least the spirit of the teaching, I ran after him, took off my sport coat, and held it out to him.

"Here," I said, "If my top coat fits you so well, maybe my sport coat will too."

He looked at me as if I were some kind of creature from another planet, snatched the sport coat from me, and hurried out the door.

I certainly never intended to give the impression that if you were generous to those who wronged you, they would repent and change right on the spot.

Like I say, I've tried it, and Christianity just doesn't work. *Did I ever say it worked? When I gave you these teachings, I wasn't giving you a lesson in how to get through life with the least damage to yourself and the things you own. I was telling you something much more important: I was telling you how to live as a son of God.*

28

The natural man protests

You Didn't Have to Make Life So Hard, God

There are so many hard things in life, God. If I had been You, when I created the world I wouldn't have made any such thing as disease. Can't You see what a difficult thing sickness is for us?

VOICE: *Do you think you could ever have appreciated good health if you hadn't been sick now and then?*

Or disasters . . . we human beings never know what's going to happen next in this world! How could You have created things like floods and fires and earthquakes? We can't feel safe one moment of our lives!

If life had always been perfectly safe, you might be complaining now because it was too boring.

Or death . . . I certainly wouldn't have made such a terrible thing as death.

What would you suggest instead of death — everyone going on living on this earth forever?

If I had made this world, I would have made things steady and dependable. I would have made the sea calm for those who must sail upon it, and the seasons come gently with no fierce heat or cold.

And what happens to people for whom everything comes too easily? Usually they're like spoiled children.
I would have made life easy and predictable. I would have made it so we wouldn't have to spend so much time looking after the sick, helping those in distress, and taking care of people with all sorts of other troubles that never should have happened in the first place. Then we could have spent all our time on ourselves!

I hate to think of what a bunch of selfish people you would have been then.
Doesn't that sound a lot better than the way You've got things set up, God?

Frankly, no. Although you must admit that man brings many of these hard things upon himself.
I hope you'll consider these criticisms seriously. With just a little thought, You could really improve this world.

With just a little thought, you might see that there's sometimes a purpose behind these things.

IF YOU'D ONLY LISTEN TO ME, GOD !

The natural man
speaks his mind

I Don't Like the Cross

I don't like the cross, God. I mean, did You have to have Jesus put to death in such a cruel way? If You wanted us to know that You love us, why didn't You just have Him go around and *tell* people? We would have believed Him.

> VOICE: *For many years My prophets had been going around telling people that I loved them. But people couldn't seem to get the idea from just words. I had to show them.*

I realize that when Jesus went to the cross, He was paying for our sin. But really, I don't feel that I'm so sinful that something *that* drastic was necessary! Couldn't You have just had Him whipped and spit on and crowned with the crown of thorns? Wouldn't that have satisfied Your demands for justice?

> *Would it have satisfied yours? Could you really have believed that your sin was paid for by the Son of God's merely being mocked and whipped?*

32

Well, after the whipping You could have had Him go out to the wilderness and spend the rest of His life peacefully teaching about God's kingdom.

I had already sent many teachers over the years. A few people listened to them. But the things they taught could never get through to the people as could one great act of love.

I'LL NEVER UNDERSTAND THAT CROSS BIT!

*The natural man
through the week*

I Don't Have Time to Read the Bible

MONDAY: The start of another busy week. I don't have time to read the Bible today.

TUESDAY: Today is even busier than yesterday!

WEDNESDAY: The work sure can pile up! No time at all today.

THURSDAY: Man, this rat race never lets up! There isn't time for Bible reading on a day like this.

FRIDAY: Friday is always such a busy day. No time today, either.

SATURDAY: Saturday again! There are so many things to take care of before the weekend. I'll never be able to squeeze in any time for Bible reading.

SUNDAY: Read the Bible today? I have to have one day a week to relax!

The natural man asks

WHY SHOULD I PRAISE GOD?

Praise the Lord!
I suppose I should praise God more.
    For it is good to sing praises to our God;
I mean, I know He wants us to.
    For he is gracious, and a song of praise is seemly.
But why should I praise Him just because He wants me to?
    He determines the number of the stars,
I mean, I know He's great and mighty —
    He gives to all of them their names.
And that He made this whole world in the first place.
    He heals the brokenhearted,
And that He's like a good father to us.
    And binds up their wounds.
And He takes care of us.
    Sing to the Lord with thanksgiving;
But why should He expect us to praise Him just because
He's done all this?
    The Lord takes pleasure in those who fear him.

I mean, doesn't that make Him sound selfish, giving us these things, then demanding that we praise Him for them?

Praise the Lord, O Jerusalem!

What? You mean the Bible doesn't *command* us to praise God? The psalmist just *invites* us to?

Praise the Lord!

But I thought —

IT'S HARD TO PRAISE SOMEONE OTHER THAN ME !

The natural man
puffs up with pride

IF ONLY EVERYONE WERE LIKE ME . . .

> *Blessed is the man who walks not in the counsel of the*
> *wicked*

I never do anything like that.

> *Nor stands in the way of sinners*

I never do things like that either.

> *Nor sits in the seat of scoffers*

Well, hardly ever.

> *But his delight is in the law of the Lord*

The Bible really is a wonderful book.

> *And on his law he meditates day and night*

Some day, after I retire, I'm really going to take time to read
the Bible.

> *He is like a tree planted by streams of water, that yields*
> *its fruit in its season*

That sounds like a slow process.

> *And its leaf does not wither*

Leaves? Fruit?

In all that he does, he prospers.
Now that's the part I like!
The wicked are not so, but are like chaff which the wind drives away.
Serves them right.
Therefore the wicked will not stand in the judgment, nor sinners in the congregation of the righteous
It's nice to know that God is going to give them what's coming to them.
For the Lord knows the way of the righteous, but the way of the wicked will perish
I'm glad You know which of us are righteous, God. If only everyone were as good as I am.

I'M GLAD I'M RIGHTEOUS!

The natural man
examines his status

I Deserve All I Have

God, I realize that the reason I have things so good is not that I'm better than other people.

I mean, just because I have a good education, good health, a loving family, and live in a free country — I know that I don't have all these things because I'm so worthy compared to other people in the world.

I mean, take the refugees around the world. They have no real home, not much to live on. Of course, they may not have worked as hard as I have. Or as hard as my father worked, or his father before him.

If those refugees had had something going like our family's hardware business, they wouldn't have just picked up and left it all behind and gone off looking for some place else to live.

If a person works hard and uses his head, he can usually come out pretty well. Of course, our area has never been hit by hurricanes or floods or earthquakes or anything.

THANKS GOD, BUT <u>I</u> DO DESERVE MY SUCCESS

But that just goes to show how wise my grandfather was to pick this town as the place to set up the business. And how wise he was to pick this country to immigrate to. If other people's ancestors chose countries that have not become as prosperous or as free as ours — or if they never got out of the old country — well, whose fault is it but their own?

And then, too, I know that we really can't say that You're on our side, God. That would be presumptuous. But doesn't it make some difference to You that ours is a Christian country? I mean, don't You make the sun shine a little brighter here and the rain fall a little more regularly? Haven't we earned the right to extra blessings?

So I thank You that I have so much, God. I feel sorry for all those around the world who have less. But that's life.

The natural man
gives himself
a pat on the back

IN PRAISE OF NORTHERN VIRTUE

Let us now sing words in praise of Northern virtue.

Up here we let the Negroes vote. We allow their children to go to our public schools. We don't worry them with the Ku Klux Klan. And we don't burn their churches. We treat them like people.

We let them live among us — with some restrictions, of course. And we offer them a wide choice of jobs — not a full choice, but quite a few jobs are open to them.

We serve them at our barber shops and our beauty shops — well, at some of them. And we let them into our churches and clubs — into the ones that we let them into, anyway. And into our colleges and universities — with a few exceptions, naturally.

Up here we welcome Negroes as neighbors — a number of us. And we invite those we have gotten to know into our homes — at least we intend to some day, when we get around to it. We consider them our social equals — on quite a few occasions.

Up here we treat Negroes like people.

The South could certainly take a lesson from us.

43

The natural man
points a finger

THOSE MONKS!

For sheer stupidity, you can't beat the monk in the Middle Ages. He lived in a little windowless room in an old monastery and spent his day working with the other monks, praying with the other monks, eating with the other monks, meditating with the other monks, talking with the other monks. He never got out to see what was going on in the world — never knew — probably never even cared. He was content in his own little ingrown world.

> VOICE: *Maybe his world was not so little. It included the God of all creation. And it included his prayers for the world.*

But he still didn't live at all like we Christians live today. Look at how we mix with the world —

> *Mix with the world? I haven't heard you being friendly with a non-Christian for a long time.*

Well, we're supposed to be separate from the world. Anyway, today we're more aware of what's going on in the world than the monks were, and we take a more active part in making a Christian impact on it.

Fine. Give me an example of something of this sort you've been doing lately.

Well . . . I mean, as Christians today we realize how important it is to bring our Christianity out of the monastery and into the world.

Like to your next-door neighbor — what's his name?

I don't know. I never met him. You see what I mean, though, don't you? How things have improved since the Middle Ages?

WE SHOULD MIX WITH THE WORLD

The natural man
speaks out

THE NATURAL MAN TAKES UP HIS CROSS . . . SORT OF

It's hard on a Christian to take up his cross. Like the other day when I had that headache. A headache's a real cross to bear.

> VOICE: *That was the day you were going to help at the clinic for migrant workers.*

Yes, but of course I couldn't, not with that headache. And then take the matter of Lenten services — I went all during Lent — only missed twice. You've got to admit that that's taking up my cross.

> *In what way?*

Well . . . I went, didn't I? There were a lot of other things I could have been doing.

> *You weren't helped by going? You didn't draw closer to God?*

Look, I went all during Lent — that was my cross. And then there are all the irritations I have to put up with every day — teachers calling on me when I haven't done my homework, coach tightening up on our training rules, a rainy day right after I've washed the car. Boy, I take up my cross every day.

These things are your cross? When I said to take up your cross and follow Me, they weren't exactly what I had in mind.

A perspective on race

THE NATURAL MAN SOLVES THE RACE PROBLEM

It's so simple, actually.

It all came to me this noon as I was eating lunch and looking out the window and I saw this Negro man about twenty-five years old go by with a little Negro boy about two or two-and-a-half years old.

And it hit me just like that! All at once I knew what we could do to end all this racial trouble! It's so simple, really — I don't know why I didn't think of it long ago.

It's this: all we would have to do would be to prevent Negroes from having any more children.

Can't you see how effectively this would solve the problem — in eighteen more years we would have no more trouble over the desegregation of schools. All the Negroes who are now children would have finished their schooling by then.

And in twenty-two more years we could quit worrying about getting more colleges open to Negroes — all the Negroes would be through college by then.

And eventually, say in 75 years or so, our problem would

be entirely solved — there'd be no more Negroes around to cause any more problems.

Isn't that a good solution?

VOICE: *Well . . . I was thinking . . . you might want to try a variation of it: you could prevent white people from having any more children.*

Prevent white people from having children! Look, we're Americans, and we have a Constitution, and that Constitution guarantees us the right to life, liberty, and the pursuit of happiness — and nobody's going to tell me I can't have children! Nobody! If you think you can —

Aren't Negroes Constitutionally-protected Americans too?

Look — if you can't be reasonable about this —

*The natural man's
mind wanders*

I Say the Apostles' Creed in Church

*I believe in God the Father Almighty, Maker of Heaven
and earth*
I wonder how many times in my life I've said the Apostles'
Creed?
And in Jesus Christ his only Son our Lord
Every time I say it, though, it gets more meaningful.
*Who was conceived by the Holy Ghost, Born of the
Virgin Mary, Suffered under Pontius Pilate*
I must have been saying it for about fifteen years now.
Was crucified, dead, and buried
Let's see — fifteen times 52 . . .
He descended into hell
Did I say 'ascended' or 'descended'? Let me think — 'de'
means 'from' or 'down' . . .
*The third day he rose again from the dead; He ascended
into Heaven*
There — 'ascended.' Got it right this time!

And sitteth on the right hand of God the Father Almighty: From thence he shall come to judge the quick and the dead

Where was I? Oh, yes — 15 times 52. Uh — 10 times 52 is 520, add half of that . . .

I believe in the Holy Ghost; The holy Christian Church 520 plus 260 equals 780 . . .

The Communion of Saints; The Forgiveness of sins; The Resurrection of the body

Just think — I've said the Apostles' Creed 780 times!

And the Life everlasting. Amen.

And every time I say it, it gets more meaningful.

The natural man
gets one-upped

THE SPECTER AND I

I had a visitor last night — in my imagination, anyway. Shortly after nightfall a dark specter entered the room.

"I have come to rid you of your father and mother," it said in a low voice.

"*Rid* me! Of my father and mother! O no! Please! Don't do anything to them!"

"You mean you care?"

"Well, of course! Please! *Please* don't!"

"But I thought you wouldn't mind. I've heard you complain about them so much that I thought here was an easy place to fill up my day's quota. Just this morning I heard you grumbling about how hard they were to live with. Well, then . . . I'll just have them injured in an accident I'm cooking up down at the corner. Let's see . . . we'll have your father lose the use of one of his legs . . . and your mother . . . let's see . . . we'll have her face marred so that she no longer looks like the same person . . . ."

BUT I AM CONCERNED !

"O no! Please! I love them!"

"I had no idea you cared."

"But —"

"I can't remember ever hearing you express any thankfulness for them . . ."

"But —"

"Well, I have a few other quotas to fill yet today. Let's see . . . I can have the gas main leak under your house, there'll be an explosion, your house will catch fire and burn to the ground, and . . ."

"No . . . please!"

"Or that friend of yours, Roger — he's going on that plane trip. We'll have something happen to the landing gear and he'll be —"

"No — *please!*"

"No? Well, then — I've got one more disaster to find a place for — a case of incurable cancer. We'll give the incurable cancer . . . to you."

"No! *Please!*"

"Well, you're certainly a fine one! Here I've been saving you for a day like this when I couldn't fill my quotas —"

"But why *me?*"

"Because you don't seem to appreciate any of the things you have — not your family, or your friends, or your home, or your health. I thought it would be easy to unload the calamities I couldn't find places for onto you. I thought you might even be glad to be rid of some of these things, the way you complain about them. There's no figuring some people!" it said, wrapped its dark robes more tightly about itself, and disappeared.

The natural man
admits a few things

JESUS' LIFE MIGHT HAVE GONE SOMETHING LIKE THIS IF HE HAD BEEN MORE LIKE ME

AT AGE 10: Why should I go to school and work so hard studying the Scriptures? There'll probably never be any chance to make use of what I learn anyway.

AT AGE 20: There's no future in working so hard here in the carpenter shop. What good will muscle and strength ever do Me?

AT AGE 30: God seems to want Me to preach, and I guess the people do, too, but I've never prepared for anything like that — I don't know enough about the Scriptures. Besides, traveling around all the time preaching would be too strenuous — I'm not strong enough for that kind of a life. Sorry.

The natural man's prayers
clog the computers

THE INTERNATIONAL GEOPRAYERICAL YEAR

Things had not been working out too well with the new electronic computer system for receiving prayers in heaven, what with the population explosion and all.

Andronius, the angel in charge of the Prayer Receiving Department, called in the thirty angels on his staff.

"Things have been piling up around here over the last few months," he began, indicating with a wave of his long sleeve the stacks of papers overflowing file drawers, tipping from tables, spilling out of racks, leaning in wild disarray against the wall. "I think you'll agree that it's about time we did something about all this."

His angelic colleagues nodded.

"What I had in mind," he proceeded, "was that we should take a year off and get all these papers filed away and maybe work some of the kinks out of our new computer system. Things have gotten a little out of hand — we need a free year to catch up."

"Take a year off! But how could we?" asked Marcus, the youngest angel on the staff. "We can't just close up the department! People need us! Every day we receive prayers of the most urgent nature! We can't just ignore people for a whole year!"

"Well, I wasn't thinking of closing down completely," Andronius explained. "I thought that perhaps we could spare one of you to handle the really urgent messages."

"One of us!" Marcus exclaimed, adjusting his waist rope. "How could one of us possibly handle all the incoming prayers?"

"Marcus, when you've worked here longer," Andronius explained gently, "when you've worked here longer, you'll realize how much of a formality most people's prayers are. Take the batch we received today." He picked up a pile of papers.

"Look at them. Here's one from Albertus McCloy. For sixty years Mr. McCloy has been saying 'Now I Lay Me Down to Sleep' every night before he gets into bed. Just that four-liner and nothing more! Sixty years! Think of how many thousands of times he's said those same few paltry words! And only once — only once! — did he really think about what he was saying: the night he was tossing and turning on his hospital bed, waiting to have his appendix out the next morning.

"And here's one from Elsietta Fronch: 'Bless Mommy and Daddy and help me be a good girl.' A charming prayer, but Elsietta's been saying it now for close to forty years.

"And look at this stack — these are the prayers offered by the members of St. Francis on the Freeway Community Church during their morning worship service last Sunday. Out of 632 worshipers during the three services, only 27 went so far as to realize anything of what they were saying.

"So," he tossed the stack of papers back onto the desk, "I think you can see why we need to get things a little

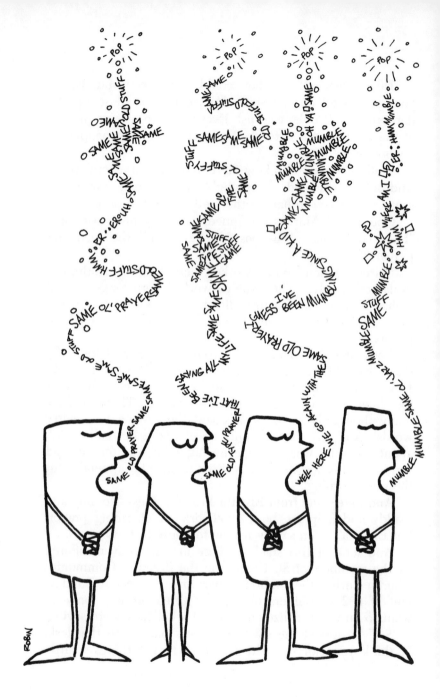

better organized around here to handle more quickly the vast quantities of junk mail — er, unmeant prayers — that we receive. And I think you can also see that one angel — even a new man — new angel, that is — on our staff will easily be able to handle all the world's prayers that matter."

"But how?" Marcus was still worried about the whole thing.

"Easy. You can put the prayers of all those who are really in earnest about what they're saying right through to the Father. The rest can be shunted onto the voice-o-type machine that we're having installed — although I don't know why we want to save them.

"But, anyway, it will take voice messages and translate them into phonetic marks on paper. It may be here tomorrow — I hope. Once it's in operation, you on my staff won't have to listen to and record the endless backwash of meaningless prayers that surges in here every time bedtime or Sunday morning touches a new part of the world."

A wild cheer went up from the assembled angels.

"Of course you all realize," he cautioned, "that in time this will mean that most of you will be out of jobs. If Marcus here can handle the whole operation by himself as soon as we get the new machine, you can see that when the rest of you get all the back work caught up, that's it."

Marcus still looked a little dubious about the whole thing, but the rest of the angels looked delighted.

"All right then, men — angels — as soon as the voice-o-type arrives, Marcus will take over the current operations and the rest of us will get the place into shape."

Another wild cheer split the air of heaven.

And thus began the International Geoprayerical Year.

The natural woman saves
wear and tear on her Bible

The Day Mrs. Shrdlu Fumbled Her Featherduster

One blustery November morning Mrs. Shrdlu was dusting her book shelf. She had grown so weary of pulling out books, flipping off the dust, and shoving them in again that she suddenly fumbled her featherduster and knocked her Bible open onto the floor.

"Mercy!" she exclaimed and sat down on the piano bench to regain her equilibrium.

It felt good to sit down and rest after so strenuous a morning. She brushed her hair back out of her eyes and looked around at the nearly clean book shelf, then down at the Bible.

She was very proud of how well she had kept her Bible — until this unfortunate accident. She had been a member of the church for thirty-seven years now, and through all these years she had had the same Bible. She was proud of that fact — that she had taken such good care of her Bible. To protect it from wear and tear was her chief concern.

It was beginning to fray a little, especially where the friction of opening and closing it had taken its toll along the binding. But Mrs. Shrdlu had prudently prolonged its life by only opening it on special occasions — like when the leader of the Bible study at some meeting would ask that they find, say, I Thessalonians 3:5.

(Except that this was another place where she saved wear and tear. She never had quite gotten around to learning where the different books of the Bible were, so whenever the leader called for any reference other than Genesis, Psalms, Matthew, Mark, Luke, John, or Revelation, her copy of the Bible was given further reprieve from use.)

And thus Mrs. Shrdlu and her Bible had gone gracefully through the years together, neither disturbing the other unduly.

Now, as the Bible lay open on the floor, her eyes caught the beginning of a chapter, and, without realizing what she was doing, she picked it up and began reading. Absorbed, she read and read.

When the telephone rang fifteen minutes later, Mrs. Shrdlu was startled to see that she had been reading the Bible — all by herself — and understanding it! She had even read so far that she had had to turn a page.

"Mercy!" she exclaimed, suddenly realizing that all this reading and page turning would wear out her Bible prematurely.

Carefully, so as not to put undue strain on the binding, she closed the Bible and put it back on the shelf.

"Mercy!" she said to herself as she went to answer the phone. "I shall have to be a little more careful with my featherduster!"

*The natural man
makes another discovery*

When the What Is Called Up Yonder

Petronius stood with his weight on one foot, then on the other. The line ahead of him was moving so slowly that it would be ages before he got his turn at the Judgment Seat.

Then he pricked up his nose. What was that delicious smell?

He leaned out of line and saw an angel coming along the line carrying a tray of hot buttered rolls, holding out the tray to each person.

Petronius had been standing in line so long that he was very hungry. And in a few moments the angel would be offering him a —

Then he suddenly realized — he must not take a roll. All his life (and he had been a Christian for as long as he could remember) he had done his best to avoid being carried away by pleasure. He had seen too many people live only for their own enjoyment and had made up his mind that he would not be one of them. For years, therefore, he had deliberately

IT'S TOUGH TO IGNORE LIFE ◻

ignored pleasurable things in order to concentrate his attention more fully on serving God.

Now the man ahead of him was taking a roll.

And now the angel was holding out the tray to Petronius. The fresh, warm, yeasty smell assailed his nostrils. His mouth began to water. He reached out his hand, then rallied himself enough to pull it back and give the angel an almost convincing, "No, thank you."

The angel moved on to the next person.

The rolls had been almost too much of a temptation. For a moment he had almost weakened and taken one, but years of self-discipline had come to his rescue at this crucial time. And it was crucial: perhaps this was a test . . . perhaps this was one of God's ways of separating the sheep from the goats. Petronius felt better as he thought of this. He had passed the test!

The line moved ahead little by little.

Now a bird began singing in a tree near him. Petronius looked until he located a small blue bird on a leafy branch above him. Never had he heard a more beautiful song. Then he turned his head away — one must not get wrapped up in the pleasures of life!

Now, as the line moved forward, he found himself opposite a large bed of red flowers. Their fragrance was sweet but fresh. He started over to examine them more closely, then caught himself; one must not be too attracted by beautiful things.

The line moved along slowly.

Now he felt something brushing against his leg and looked down to see a small yellow-and-white kitten. "Mew!" the kitten said, looking up into Petronius's face, and rubbed its back against his ankle. Petronius had to employ all his self-restraint to keep from reaching down and picking up the kitten; his years of giving up pleasurable things once again shored him up.

The line inched slowly forward.

Then at last the man ahead of him stepped to the side and Petronius found that he was the one before the Judgment Seat. The Judgment Seat!

He shut his eyes and knelt in wonder and awe.

After many moments he felt God's hand upon his shoulder and heard God saying, "Well done, my son. I am glad you have come home. You have served me faithfully and well; you have been a most loving son. There is just one thing, however."

Here God took Petronius's hand and lifted him to a standing position. Petronius opened his eyes and saw in the air behind God's throne a series of moving pictures. He saw himself as he had lived his life on earth from day to day — grim, tense, unbending, unappreciating. And he saw the cold, unloving effect it had had on those around him. Then he heard God speaking again:

"My son, did you not know that I created all the good things of the earth for you to enjoy? I wanted you to love Me and serve Me, but I also wanted you to enjoy the good things I made for you."

Then Petronius noticed that God had something on His lap — a small yellow-and-white kitten — the same kitten that Petronius had so carefully avoided picking up. He noticed too that God was taking a moment to enjoy listening to a small blue bird singing in the branches above Him.

On the table next to God's throne he noticed a vase of the fragrant red flowers that he had forced himself to ignore. And a plate with a half-eaten roll.

Now in the air behind the throne he watched these words appear: "A man will have to give account on Judgment Day for all the good things he refused to enjoy when he might have done so."

Petronius knelt before God once more, then hurried out.

"Angel —" he called, running down the long line. "Angel — a roll, please."

The natural man
gets his come-uppance

The Empty Chair Affair

As the family sat down to supper, Linus McKimbo looked at his son's empty chair.

"It'll be strange having Bill off to college," he said. "Doesn't seem like just this morning we took him down to old State."

"I suppose it'll take us a while to get used to the empty place at the table," his wife added. "There've been five of us for so many years now."

When everyone was seated, they repeated together the prayer they said before every meal, "Come, Lord Jesus, Be Our Guest."

Before the "Amen" finished echoing across the room, Larry, 12, helped himself to a generous serving of fried chicken and Anne, 9, scooped mashed potatoes onto her plate.

Mrs. McKimbo took some tossed salad and passed it on to Larry.

Only Linus McKimbo sat motionless, his eyes fixed on the empty chair. He shut his eyes and opened them again. It was still there.

How could this be? Could he really be seeing what he thought he was seeing? Things like this just didn't happen!

He thought back over the words of the prayer they had just said. But no — the One they had just asked to come wouldn't *really* come — would He?

He decided it must be his nerves — he had been working pretty hard lately.

He shut his eyes and opened them again. The Guest was still there.

Then he wondered: if he could see Him, maybe some of the other members of the family could too. He looked around the table. All of them were busy filling their plates and passing serving dishes.

He managed to catch his wife's eye and tried, without saying anything, to direct her attention to the empty chair — or to the chair that had been empty — until now.

He made a slight motion with his head toward the chair and waited for her reaction. She looked at him quizzically for a moment, then went back to cutting her chicken. He caught her eye again and this time made a motion with his right shoulder toward the chair.

"Linus!" she said. "Whatever is the matter with you? You haven't eaten a thing! You don't even have a thing on your plate! Here —" she passed him the chicken — "try some of your favorite white meat."

Mechanically he took a piece and put it on his plate.

"And here — have some potatoes and salad."

He took the food and served himself without letting his eyes stray completely from the chair.

"Linus! Whatever is the matter with you?" She put down her fork and looked at him.

He tried once more to get her to look at the chair. He

looked squarely into her eyes, then shifted his gaze deliberately toward the chair. Quickly he looked back. She was looking at the chair!

"Why, Linus," she said, "I think you're homesick for Bill already!" She reached out and touched his hand.

She had looked right at the chair — and she hadn't seen anything but an empty chair!

Linus McKimbo checked again . . . the Guest was still there. And apparently no one else in the family could see Him! The Guest was there, just as they had asked Him to be, and he was the only one who knew it!

"Linus, try to eat something. You can't just sit there and brood over Bill being gone."

He tried a bite of chicken, but his mind wasn't on food. Couldn't anyone else see their Guest? Couldn't anyone else see that He had come, just as they had asked, and was sitting right there with them?

Now a neighbor passed by on the sidewalk.

"Look!" Larry exclaimed, looking out the window. "There goes mean old Mr. Zingler!"

"Larry," Mr. McKimbo said evenly, trying to make his own righteousness obvious to the Guest, "we shouldn't talk about anyone like that."

"Why? You always call him 'mean old Mr. Zingler.'"

Linus McKimbo cleared his throat violently.

"Whoops!" Anne said. "You scared me!" Milk was soaking into the tablecloth in front of her. "You coughed so loud just as I was picking up my glass that I spilled my milk!"

"That's all right, honey."

"You aren't mad, Daddy? Aren't you mad at me for spilling my milk? Usually you roar at me!"

"Well . . ." Linus McKimbo cleared his throat again, glancing out of the corner of his eye at the non-vacant chair, "Well . . ."

"And you haven't complained about the chicken," his wife

70

put in half teasingly. "Usually it's too salty or overdone or underdone or something. You haven't roared at any of us tonight!"

"Well . . . I . . ." He did not quite dare look toward the chair any more.

"Well, eat anyway," his wife said brightly. "Give your homesickness for Bill something to work with."

He ate halfheartedly.

And then his wife was bringing in the dessert — strawberry shortcake.

His appetite returned a little, but not enough for him to finish the hearty portion his wife served him. But no one seemed to notice. The rest of the family dug into their dessert with gusto.

"Mama, may I go down and play with Kathy?" Anne asked when all her shortcake was gone.

"As soon as you and I are through with dishes."

"I'm going over to work on model cars with Fred," Larry said as he swung his jacket on.

The next thing Linus McKimbo knew, the family had gotten up from the table. He glanced cautiously toward the chair. It was empty. He looked again. There was definitely no one in it. He walked over and touched it to make sure.

"Linus," his wife said tenderly, "if it's going to bother you so much to have Bill gone, I'll move that chair into the living room. There's no need to have an empty chair at the table. We can always bring it back if we have a guest."

"Yes," Linus McKimbo repeated slowly, "if we have a guest."

The natural man
begins to appreciate
the privilege of praying

I Had a Little Trouble Praying

I had a little trouble praying last night. Scarcely had I said, "Dear Father," when an angelic voice inquired, "What number is calling?"

"What *number*? I'm praying!"

"Yes. What is your number, please."

"*What* number?"

"A card was mailed to you several days ago giving your number," the voice said crisply.

"Card? Oh — do you mean that green piece of cardboard with all the holes punched in it?"

"That is correct. Will you refer to it now, please? If you will give me the number from the lower left hand corner of the card, I will be ready to switch your call to our electronic computer and you may begin recording your message for processing." The voice had all the warmth of an abandoned hamburger.

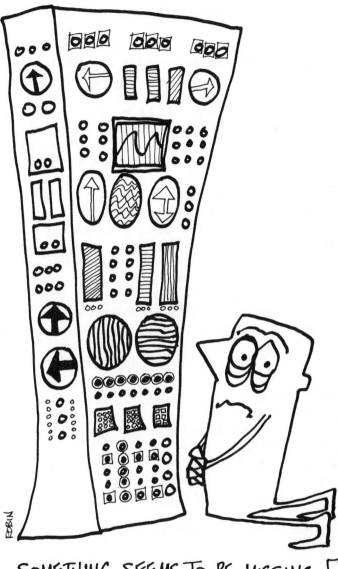

SOMETHING SEEMS TO BE MISSING !

"Recording? You mean I don't get to talk directly to God?"

"We're changing over the whole system. For the present, calls will be handled and processed by our staff, but as soon as the operation becomes fully automated, things will be strictly between you and the IBM machine."

"I see. Well —" How could I begin? How could I speak words of worship and praise into a pile of levers and gears? But if this was the way it was — "I would like to ask God to be with my friend Louise who just left on the train for Chicago," I began hesitantly.

"What is her number, please?"

"Number? I don't know her number!"

"Could you give us a description of her, please?"

"Well, she's nineteen, has blonde hair, green eyes, is 5'6" and weighs about 120, and she's knitting a white cardigan sweater in a large cable stitch."

"Which train is she on, please?"

"Which train . . . I think it's the Illinois Central."

"Could you give me the exact location of the train at the present moment?"

"Look, all I know is that it's due in Chicago about seven tomorrow morning."

"And her name is Louise?"

"Yes, Louise Peterson."

"How do you spell the last name?"

"P-E-T-E-R-S-O-N."

"P as in 'perpendicular'?"

"Yes."

"But you don't know her number."

"No."

"We will try to process this, but you realize that without her number —"

"Yes, yes." The whole thing was becoming exasperating.

"If you have no more petitions, I will switch you to the

department that processes adoration," the voice said. "From there you will be connected with the department that processes forgiveness. When you hear the three electronic bells, you may begin your message. Are there any questions?"

"Well . . . I . . ."

"Wait for the three bells, then begin your message." There was a click as she (he? it?) hung up.

The first of the mechanical bells sounded. Its sterile iciness chilled my blood.

Without waiting for the next two, I got up from my knees, climbed into bed, and turned off the light. Sometimes things go just a little too far.

The natural man shudders
at man's inhumanity

NUCLEAR THOUGHT

This day may lack the usual sequel
If all men are cremated equal.

76

The natural man
makes another discovery

High Noon in Heaven

I dreamt I died and went to heaven. It was morning. St. Peter with his long beard and turtle neck sweater met me at the gate. He was most friendly.

"Go right on in," he said.

I was a little bewildered. "Where do I go?"

"Well, I imagine you'll want to see the Father first," he said. "Walk straight down this street and you'll come to a large building — you can't miss it because the road ends there. And here," he thrust a piece of paper into my hand, "take this with you. It may be helpful when you get there."

I thanked him and began walking down the road. As I walked, a small, light brown, furry animal about the size of a chipmunk kept pace with me in the grass along the road, now running ahead, now crossing over to the other side behind me.

From a large clump of purple flowers of some variety I had never seen before a delicate fragrance perfumed the air.

78

High in the branches above me a small yellow bird sang a beautiful melody.

But, the farther I walked, the more I began to wonder: so far I had not seen a single person. Perhaps this was some high day in heaven, I told myself, and everyone had gathered somewhere in celebration. But wouldn't there have been someone around somewhere?

After what seemed half an hour or more, I finally arrived at the large building at the end of the street. The large, heavily-carved door was opened for me by an angel, as was each successive door, until I found myself before a great golden door.

The angels beside it stepped back. Hesitantly I put my hand on the handle of the great door. Almost by itself it opened.

Inside, dazzled and blinded by the light from the throne, I dropped to my knees and covered my face with my hands.

A great while later I took my hands from my face when I heard God speaking to me.

"At last you're here," He said. "I've been waiting for you."

He'd been waiting for me!

Now, with my eyes open, I saw that He was not sitting on a throne as I had thought at first, but on a large, rough rock. Below Him the planet that I had always referred to as Earth turned slowly.

He motioned for me to get up and stand before Him. As I stood facing Him, there were so many things I wanted to say to Him — so many things I wanted to ask Him.

But foremost in my mind was the question that had plagued me ever since I entered heaven: Where was everyone? It seemed like too trifling a thing to mention at a time like this, but my curiosity had gotten the better of me; I had to find out.

"Where in the world is everyone?" I asked, then decided to rephrase it. "Where is everyone?"

"Everyone?" God asked. "What do you mean by 'everyone'?"

"The people. All the people I knew on earth who died and came here. I haven't seen anyone at all since I got here. Where are they?"

Here God leaned back against the rock and seemed to be searching for words. His answer was so long in coming that I began to fidget. The palms of my hands grew damp; as I unclasped my right hand, the piece of paper St. Peter had given me fell to my feet. I picked it up, unfolded it, and read: "Truly, I say to you, as you did it to one of the least of these my brethren, you did it to me."

I wondered why St. Peter had thought that these words would be helpful. They were certainly familiar — I had read them many times on earth — but helpful at this particular time?

Now God was speaking. "You ask where everyone is," He said. "Everyone . . ." The word seemed to have a special meaning to Him. "Did you not know," He said slowly, "that there was no one on earth but you and Me?"

The natural man
puts his feet
in someone else's shoes

Black Thought

If I had been born black
Would I consider myself inferior?
Would I be willing to live as a not-quite person,
Making no protest to injustice,
To injury,
To insult . . .
Working my way to a doctor's degree in electrical engineer-
    ing to take a job changing worn-out light bulbs in a
    department store . . .

If I had been born black
Would I be silent when doors were shut before me . . .
Would I have no part in the sit-ins, the marches, the
    demonstrations . . .
Would I want no revenge when children were hurt . . .

Would I peer calmly out the window at the fires in the
    night . . .
Would I have the patience to wait
If I had been born black?

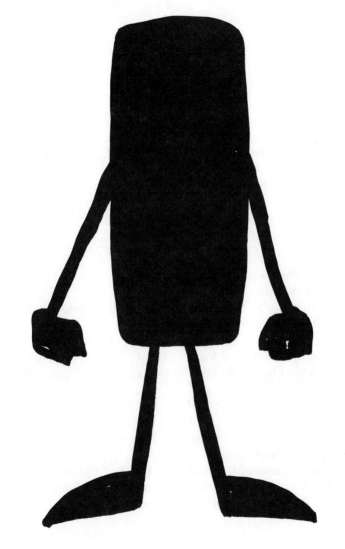

*The natural man remembers
the Russian astronaut's
report that he did not
find God in outer space*

OUR FATHER WHO ART . . .

Our Father who art right here,
Closer than breathing,
Did the man in the space capsule really expect to see You
when he reached outer space?
Did he think of You as sitting way out there somewhere
in a seeable form, in a form visible to his earthly eyes? Did
he think that he would be able to sneak up and get a glimpse
of You?
Where is heaven, God? Out past even the farthest point
in space that man will ever be able to probe? Or closer in
. . . much closer . . . so close that the earth itself may even
be superimposed upon it . . .
Oh God, unseeable Creator of the vast universe, replace,
in this day of our expanding knowledge of Your universe,
our small ideas of You with larger ones.

The natural man
realizes his imperfections

Eight Years As a Third Cornet

I think I possibly hold some kind of a record. (Actually I am a little tired of holding it, so if you know of someone who can rightfully take it off my hands, let me know and I will readily relinquish it.)

I think I am possibly the only person who has spent eight years in a school band as a third cornet.

You know how it all works: a beginning cornetist, when he has attained proficiency sufficient to allow him to add his feeble (though sometimes not feeble enough) distonations to those of musicians of longer standing, is admitted into the band and placed in what is known as the third chair. From there, as time progresses and he progresses (and better players graduate), he moves up to second cornet, then to first, then to solo.

I had to be the exception to all this. I started out as a lowly third cornet the week I enrolled in the fifth grade and held the chair through thick and thin right on through my

senior year in high school. When I graduated, the music department said it certainly was a record, but they weren't sure whether it was a 78 for barely passing or an L.P. for 'lack of progress.'

Let's face it — I somehow didn't have what it took to be a cornetist.

And, as long as we're on the subject, I suppose I may as well admit that I have also probably attained all time lows in bowling, American history, and that high and noble art, patience — to mention only a few of my numerous inadequacies. With me it's a case of "Anything you can do, I probably can't do at all." In fact, when you come right down to it, I'm sometimes a pretty mediocre human being.

Perhaps I'm not the only thing in creation that has failed to reach perfection, though. Perhaps in the scheme of things even imperfect things have their place, like the scrawny tree in the poem, "Ministry of Imperfection," a poor wreck of a tree that seemed good for nothing — too twisted to be made into lumber, hardly a thing of beauty. Yet when the snows fell on it, its gnarled arms made the snow seem even more beautiful by contrast:

> For years that stunted tree has not fulfilled
> The traits prescribed for its specific strain.
> The tortured growth, the knotty, twisted grain
> Rejects the chance it ever will be milled.
> What purpose gained, since nature's scheme has willed
> That this misshapen form shall not attain
> Beauty or usefulness? It stands a bane
> To beauty. Yet, when winter's clouds are chilled,
> And toss their pompons white and wet below,
> This is the tree on whose arthritic arms
> Snow blossoms cling and crystal clusters grow.
> Each blighted branch sustains these graceful charms
> Of perfect splendor; proves they often need
> The help of grosser patterns to succeed.*

When I think of how much better I could serve God if

* Ralph Seager, *Songs from a Willow Whistle*, (Sanbornville, New Hampshire: Wake-Brook House, 1956). Used by permission.

I were only perfect (or even somewhere remotely near it) and of how much more useful I would be in His kingdom if I could do many things (or even a few things) really well, I despair. Here I am — a perpetual third .cornet, a stunted tree.

I probably would have had my poor misshapen branches chopped up for kindling long ago if I hadn't remembered Christ's words about His strength being made perfect in weakness.

If His strength is made perfect in weakness, then perhaps He has a place for even a gnarled tree like me in the work of His kingdom.

Perhaps, by contrast, my imperfections serve to highlight His strength. Perhaps my grosser patterns serve to show His perfect splendor. Perhaps there is even a place for a stunted tree in His kingdom.

The natural man
discovers God

THE INCIDENT AT ST. DUTY'S

It was Sunday morning.

Quigula Jones climbed the steps of St. Duty's Community Church and went inside.

The interior of the church was so familiar that he hardly noticed the dark, exposed beams of the ceiling or the perpetual dampness.

This was the church in which he had been baptized as an infant, to which he had been brought regularly throughout his childhood, and to which he had come routinely ever since to fulfill his Christian duty.

(His sense of dutifulness was further reinforced by the large billboard that he passed on his way to school every morning. Erected by some local service club, the sign proclaimed in large Gothic letters, 'KEEP YOUR COUNTRY STRONG – GO TO CHURCH THIS SUNDAY!')

As the service began, Quigula sang the opening hymn a little louder than he felt like singing it, dutifully swelling

I DIG, I DIG!

the chorus that the congregation was raising to the courts above.

Dutifully he listened to the opening prayer.

Dutifully he prayed.

Dutifully he placed the offering that was larger than he really felt like giving into the offering plate.

Then it happened.

How or why it happened he could not tell, but suddenly, as he was dutifully listening to the sermon, the realization struck him: "God is!"

Stunned, he forgot to listen to the rest of the sermon, forgot to sing his best on the closing hymn, forgot to shake the minister's hand as he went exulting out the door.

"God is!" he exclaimed to the world in general as he reached the bright sunlight outside.

"God is!" he declaimed to a fellow church member and shook his hand.

"God is!" he proclaimed to a tiny girl, patting her on the head.

Dutifully the churchgoers going down the steps with him ignored his sudden indiscretions. Dutifully they avoided looking at him. Dutifully they pretended they had not heard him. Such behavior as his was certainly out of place at St. Duty's Community Church.